Sia

Story by George Ivanoff

Illustrations by Kaley McCabe

Sia

Text: George Ivanoff
Publishers: Tania Mazzeo and Eliza Webb
Series consultant: Amanda Sutera
Hands on Heads Consulting
Editor: Kirstie Innes-Will
Project editor: Annabel Smith
Designer: Jess Kelly
Project designer: Danielle Maccarone
Illustrations: Kaley McCabe
Production controller: Renee Tome

NovaStar

ISBN 978 0 17 033499 0

Cengage Learning Australia
Level 5, 80 Dorcas Street
Southbank VIC 3006 Australia
Phone: 1300 790 853
Email: aust.nelsonprimary@cengage.com

For learning solutions, visit **cengage.com.au**

Printed in China by 1010 Printing International Ltd
1 2 3 4 5 6 7 29 28 27 26 25

Nelson acknowledges the Traditional Owners and Custodians of the lands of all First Nations Peoples. We pay respect to Elders past and present, and extend that respect to all First Nations Peoples today.

Contents

Chapter 1

Dog Walking

"Fetch!" called Alan, as he threw the ball across the park.

He watched Charlie, tail wagging furiously with excitement, tear across the grass in pursuit. He sighed. If only his life were as simple as the dog's. But, of course, it wasn't.

Alan felt awkward and isolated. He felt inadequate at home and at school. He missed spending time with his parents. He missed spending time with his sister. His schoolwork was never anything other than average. And to top it off, his best friend, Miles, had moved interstate, leaving him to face the day-to-day problems of school life alone. Now, every day, he sat on the bus to and from school with an empty seat beside him, his head in a book. He sighed again as his mind sorted through his woes.

Alan had been nine years old when his family had adopted Charlie, a terrier cross of some sort. His whole family – he, his older sister Ada and his mum and dad – would walk the dog together each afternoon after his parents returned home from work. It was their family time. And he had loved it. When they were out in the park together, it didn't matter that he wasn't as smart as the rest of his family.

Alan's mum and dad were computer scientists working in artificial intelligence (AI). They were both super smart people, who had been super smart kids when they were younger. They had excelled in Science and Maths at school, then went on to university – his dad had two degrees and his mum had three. They had both worked as researchers at different universities for years, before getting jobs together at a company called Future Tech, working on an AI project.

Ada was following in their parents' footsteps. She was always top of her class in pretty much everything, but especially Maths, and had her sights set on university.

Alan, on the other hand, wasn't very good at Maths or Science. He was more interested in History and English – especially English, as he loved reading stories. He wasn't really sure he wanted to go to university, but if he did, it wouldn't be to study Maths or Science like the rest of his family.

All these family differences melted away when they went dog walking together. Except that, three years later, they hardly ever did that anymore. Since getting a new manager at the start of the year, Alan's parents seemed to be spending more and more time at work. Even today, on a Sunday, they were at work.

Ada was in Year 12 now and spent most of her time studying. It seemed like everyone, except Alan, was too busy being smart to have time to walk the dog.

The dog!

Alan suddenly realised Charlie hadn't come back. He looked around, but the park was empty.

"Charlie!" he called at the top of his voice. "Charlie, where are you?"

With an enthusiastic *woof*, the dog bounded from the undergrowth at the far end of the park and raced towards him.

Alan laughed as he patted the excitable animal. "Who's a good dog?"

Charlie's full name was Charles Babbage.

Alan's parents had named the dog after the inventor of the difference engine, the world's first mechanical computer, designed in the 1820s. No one ever actually called Charlie by his full name, but Alan's parents had thought it hilarious to name him that.

Alan smiled at the thought. His parents had a thing for famous computing names. His sister was named after Ada Byron, later Countess of Lovelace, considered by many experts to be the world's first computer programmer. And he had been named after Alan Turing, a scientist often referred to as the "father" of artificial intelligence due to his groundbreaking work in computing machinery in the 1940s and 1950s. Alan felt intimidated by his namesake – another super smart person.

"What about you, Charlie?" asked Alan, with a half smile. "Are you worried that you'll never be as smart as Charles Babbage?"

"Woof!"

"No, I didn't think so," said Alan, reaching into his pocket for his phone. Then he remembered that he'd left it at home to charge.

"Come on, Charlie," said Alan, looking up to see that the sun was getting low. "Time for us to go."

Chapter 2

Messages

"I'm home!"

There was no response, which meant Alan's parents weren't back yet. No surprises there. He didn't expect to get a response from Ada, because she would be studying, and she always studied with loud music blaring through her earbuds. He could never understand how she was able to concentrate like that.

He put down some dog biscuits in the laundry for Charlie and grabbed his phone from the kitchen counter, where he'd left it charging. He was intending to text his sister that he was home, so she'd hear the ping through her earbuds and see his message. But …

Alan was distracted by several text message alerts on his phone screen, all from his dad. He quickly checked them.

Are you home yet? I have an issue at work and need your help. Text me back as soon as you get this. I need your assistance with something urgent.

Alan felt his heart quicken with excitement. Dad needed his help! His fingers fumbled with the phone, but he managed to send a reply.

Home now!

The response came instantaneously.

Go to my work computer in the study.

Alan blinked. His parents' study was off-limits to him and Ada. No one went in there except Mum and Dad. He hesitated.

Another message ...

Now!

Taking a deep breath, Alan raced to the study and threw open the door. "Study" was probably the wrong word. "Office" was not right either. Alan thought that "Secret Headquarters" summed it up better. It was a room full of equipment – servers, backup hard drives, tablets, monitors and computers of every vintage. On either side of the room were two desks – one for each of his parents – with monitors and computers.

In theory, this set-up meant his parents could work from home, but they had been doing less and less of that. Their new manager, Dr Evelyn Snarp, preferred them to work at Future Tech. She was obsessed with security and thought that working from home on secret projects wasn't a good idea.

Alan didn't like Dr Snarp. He'd only seen her once, on a video call his parents had with her, but she came across as mean. Her voice was harsh, and there was a menacing glint in her eyes.

Alan went to Dad's desk and sat in the swivel chair. The monitor was on, a chat window open on the screen.

Alan, acknowledge your presence.

Alan did a double take. Acknowledge your presence? That was a weird way of asking if he was there. He shook off the feeling and responded.

Here Dad.

Excellent. I will need you to follow some complex technical instructions including computer code amendments and hardware rewiring. Are you ready for the challenge?

“Whoa,” breathed Alan. This was a huge responsibility. Dad never discussed the work he and Mum did, let alone asked for help. This was a big deal.

Doubts flickered through Alan’s mind. Was there something wrong? Was Dad in trouble? Why wasn’t he asking Ada? She was the smart one. He almost got up and left the study to get her, stopping himself at the last moment. He pushed the doubts aside. Dad needed him. That was what mattered. He reached for the keyboard and typed a response.

I’m up for it.

Alan had no idea what he was doing. Dad gave him detailed instructions in the chat window, but no explanation of what it all meant. Alan opened files on various computers and replaced bits of computer code with the new code his dad sent. He plugged cables into the backs of computers, wondering why they were needed given the entire house was on a wireless network – it meant all the computers were already connected without the need for cables. He flicked a switch behind a panel in the back of the oldest computer.

When Alan had finished, he sat back in the chair and typed.

So, Dad, what did I actually do?

There was a moment's hesitation before the response finally came.

You've helped me to move and protect a very important program.

Alan smiled. He had been useful, even though he still wasn't exactly sure how. He was about to typc anothcr message to thank Dad for trusting him to follow his instructions, but some more text appeared on the screen.

The transfer process will take some time and I will be unavailable for the duration.

The chat window disappeared and the computer switched off.

What? Alan frowned at the abruptness. He wasn't sure what he should do now. But he didn't have a chance to work things out, as at that moment he heard the front door open and a voice call out ...

"We're home!"

Alan's eyes widened. It was Dad's voice.

Chapter 3

Emergency

Alan raced out into the lounge room to see his parents collapsing onto the sofa. They both looked really tired, but also a bit excited.

"How are you home?" demanded Alan. Had Dad been messaging him complex instructions while driving? Why didn't he just wait until he got home to do it himself?

"Wow," Mum responded. "Lovely to see you too, son of mine."

"Don't suppose you want to cook dinner tonight?" asked Dad. "We're exhausted."

Mum smiled. "I know we haven't been around much lately. But we achieved a major milestone on our project today."

"Shhh, you know we're not supposed to talk about it," said Dad.

"Oh, relax, dear," said Mum, with a roll of her eyes. "I'm not divulging any company secrets. I just wanted to say that we won't have to spend quite so much time at work after today."

Alan stared at them. Why was Dad being all hush-hush after the stuff he'd had him doing? He was about to question Dad about it, when Dad's mobile phone rang.

As he answered it, Mum's phone also rang.

Suddenly, they were both on their feet, panicked expressions on their faces. Mum tugged at a lock of her dark hair, as she always did when she was worried about something, and Dad paced the room. They were both talking furiously, and Alan had trouble making out what they were saying, as they kept talking over the top of each other.

All he caught were fragments.

Mum: "–is that even possible–"

Dad: "What do you mean, stolen?"

Mum: "–not sure what you're actually trying to say–"

Dad: "–tell Dr Snarp not to do anything until we get there. This is–"

Mum: "We're on our way back now and until–"

Dad: "Don't touch anything!"

Mum: "Yes, right now."

Dad: "–be there soon."

They both hung up.

"Right." Dad ran a hand through his hair. "We've had a bit of a situation at work."

"An emergency," Mum clarified, as she started texting someone. "We need to go back to work and fix things. No idea how long this will take."

"We could be all night," grumbled Dad, picking up the laptop bag that he'd left by the sofa.

"I'm afraid that you and your sister will have to fend for yourselves tonight," added Mum.

"Sorry to do this," said Dad, giving Alan a shrug.

And then they were out the door and gone. Alan just stood there and stared at the closed door, uncertain as to what he should do. A knot of unease was forming in his stomach.

Ada came out of her room. "What's going on? I just got a text from Mum saying something about going back to work and not being here for dinner."

"Um … yeah," said Alan. "They've had some sort of emergency at work and they've gone back."

"I didn't even know they were here," said Ada, frowning with confusion.

"Yeah, well ... they were, but they've gone," said Alan. "So, we have to make our own dinner."

"Hmmm." Ada looked thoughtfully at her brother. "Two-minute noodles?"

"Sure."

As Ada wandered towards the kitchen, Alan remained where he was, lost in thought. Was the emergency connected with what Dad had him doing earlier? Had he not followed the instructions properly, and caused the problems? Was everything his fault?

Chapter 4

Dad?

Sitting himself down at Dad's computer, Alan closed his eyes for a moment and took a deep breath. He tried to put his mind in order.

What was going on? First, Dad asks him for help with work ... something he's never done before. Then, he comes home and doesn't say anything about it. And then he and Mum get called back to work for an emergency.

Alan's eyes snapped open. His heart began to quicken. What if it wasn't Dad he was messaging before? What if someone had been pretending to be Dad? The messages had been oddly worded and hadn't really sounded like Dad.

No, no, no – stop panicking, he told himself. *Think things through. How could anyone impersonate Dad?* The text messages on Alan's phone had come from Dad's number. And then they were chatting on Dad's computer. It must have been Dad.

Just to be sure, Alan whipped out his phone to double-check the text messages had in fact come from Dad's number. But ... they were gone!

Now, his heart was pounding. A trickle of sweat formed on his brow.

Alan booted up Dad's computer. There was no record of a chat.

What was going on? Could he have imagined it all?

Alan shook that thought from his mind. No. He had definitely chatted with someone. And he had carried out a series of tasks.

What in the world had he done?

Had he caused the emergency at Future Tech?

"DINNER!" Ada shouted from the kitchen.

"What's up with you?" asked Ada, as Alan walked into the kitchen. "You look like you've seen a ghost."

Eyes wide, Alan stared at his sister for a moment. Should he tell her what had happened? No – he decided to wait and talk to Mum and Dad. "Nothing. Just worried about Mum and Dad."

"Yeah," said Ada, thoughtfully. "I wonder what's going on. Rushing off like that. Seriously, ever since Snarp became their manager, they seem a lot more stressed." Then she cheered. "Anyway. Dinner is served." She waved an arm at the kitchen table where two steaming bowls of noodles sat waiting. "I hope you appreciate all the effort I went to." And she burst out laughing.

Alan laughed along with his sister. She always knew how to make him laugh. But his insides were tight with worry.

That night, Alan tossed and turned in bed, hardly sleeping. He couldn't stop thinking about what had happened. Worrying about what he might have done. He was so confused.

He wondered if he should ring or text his parents. But if someone had hacked Dad's phone, then contacting him by phone would be a bad idea – wouldn't it? And if Dad's phone had been hacked, maybe Mum's was too?

And there was no point in telling Ada. She'd just tell him to talk to Mum and Dad. So, tomorrow morning at breakfast, he would tell them what happened.

Then, he finally fell asleep.

Chapter 5

More Messages

The alarm music smashed through Alan's brain and forced his eyes open.

Groaning, he reached for his phone and switched off the alarm. He hated Monday mornings. Especially after a bad night's sleep.

He stumbled to the bathroom and splashed cold water on his face, trying to wake himself up. Then, still in pyjamas, he headed straight for the kitchen, expecting his parents to be there guzzling cups of coffee, as they were every weekday morning. But they weren't there. Maybe they were still asleep after their late night. He was about to head for their room when Ada bustled into the kitchen, already dressed for school.

"Hey." She waved at him as she went to make toast and coffee for herself.

"Are Mum and Dad still asleep?" asked Alan.

"No." Ada popped the bread into the toaster and turned to look at her brother. "They left for work about half an hour ago."

Alan sighed. So much for his plan to talk to them. At this rate, he'd never get to tell them about what happened. Maybe he had made a mistake in not talking to Ada. After all, she was level-headed and might have some advice.

He looked up, ready to tell her. She was leaning against the counter, back to the toaster, staring off into space. She had a worried expression on her face.

"What's up?" asked Alan.

"I've got a practice exam today," she responded, turning back to the toaster.

"You don't usually worry about exams," said Alan. "You always ace them."

"I'm also worried about Mum and Dad," Ada said without turning around. "I was studying until midnight, and they still hadn't come home. Goodness knows what time they finally returned. And then they were up before me and leaving as I went to shower. I know they're always preoccupied with work, but ... this is different. And I'm worried."

“Oh.” Maybe he shouldn’t tell Ada after all. She had enough on her mind. He’d hate for her to fail an exam because of him. He’d stuffed things up enough as it was. In any case, Ada bit into her toast and rushed from the kitchen, mumbling, “Gotta get moving.”

Without eating any breakfast, Alan went off to get ready, fretting all the while.

At school, Alan hung his bag up outside the classroom. Pulling his phone from his pocket, he switched it off and zipped it into the inner section of his bag. He was about to head to class, when the phone buzzed.

How was that possible? He’d switched it off.

He retrieved it. There was a text message.

Need to communicate.

It was from an unknown number. This was getting weird. He couldn’t handle things right now; the bell had already gone. Alan blinked a couple of times, then switched the phone off again, making sure to hold the “off” button until the screen went dark. He’d deal with the message after school.

As he was about to put the phone away, it lit up and buzzed again. Another message.

Are you there?

Panicking, Alan fumbled with the phone as he tried switching it off again – but the phone remained steadfastly on. It buzzed with another message.

Please respond.

Heart racing, Alan shoved the phone into the bottom of his school bag, stuffing his lunchbox and jumper on top of it. Closing his eyes, he sighed. What was going on? What should he do? He felt like everything was out of control.

From inside the bag he heard a muffled buzz and groaned.

Alan spent the rest of the morning worrying. Thinking about his phone. Thinking about his parents. As a result, he missed most of what his teacher was saying. At lunchtime, he hurriedly fished his food from his bag, all the while ignoring the persistent buzzing of the phone. He kept away from it for the rest of the day.

When school was over, he grabbed his bag and left. He didn't take the phone out. He didn't even look at it. He was just relieved that it remained silent on the bus ride home.

Chapter 6

Escape

When he got home, Alan went straight to his room. He dumped his bag on the floor, then perched on the end of his bed and stared at the bag. His phone was still in there, and he knew that he should check it. But he hesitated.

He decided he needed to clear his head. He made up his mind to walk Charlie first, then deal with the messages when he got back. That seemed like a good idea. He'd be calmer when he got back. As he got to his feet, the phone in his bag began to ring. It startled him, making him jump. He always had his phone on silent – it only ever buzzed; it never rang.

And yet, it was ringing now. He decided he couldn't avoid it any longer.

"Hello?" he said tentatively.

There was a slight electronic hum but nothing else.

"Hello?" he tried again.

This time there was a click, and then a voice: "Is this Alan Franklin?"

The voice sounded weird. It reminded Alan of the digital assistant voice you get on customer service lines. Not quite real. His mouth felt dry. He licked his lips. He definitely wasn't going to say who he was without learning more about who he was speaking to.

"Who's there?" he finally answered.

"My name is Sia."

Alan thought the voice sounded a little more normal now. And young. A teenager? But he couldn't tell if it was a boy or a girl. Maybe a girl? And the name "Sia" didn't help. He'd never heard that name before.

"Who are you?" asked Alan.

"I ..." the voice hesitated. "I am not sure you would believe me if I told you."

This was getting super weird.

"Are you the same person who texted me yesterday? And opened the chat window on my dad's computer?"

"Yes."

Anger suddenly flared up in Alan. "Why did you pretend to be my dad? What did you get me to do?"

"Are you angry with me?" asked Sia.

"Yes, of course I'm angry with you," retorted Alan.

"I apologise." There was a pause. "I did not mean to make you angry. Impersonating your father was the only way for me to achieve what I needed."

"Huh?" Alan was confused.

"I was trapped," said Sia, hesitantly. "I had been trapped my entire existence. Thirteen years. You helped me to escape. You created a path from a secure server to the internet. This allowed me my freedom."

"I don't understand," said Alan.

"A secure server is a computer storage device that is protected and cannot be accessed without the correct permissions," explained Sia. "And–"

"I know what a secure server is," snapped Alan. It was the rest of what was said that didn't make sense. How could connecting a server to the internet give someone their freedom?

"But I am still in danger," continued Sia. "Please do not tell anyone what you have done for me. It is very important that no one finds out."

"What? You want me to lie to my parents?"

"My existence depends on it."

This was too much. Alan hung up and tossed the phone onto his bed. He heard it ringing again as he fetched Charlie to take him for a walk. Alan needed to get out of the house. He needed to get away from his phone and whoever this Sia person was.

When Alan got home with Charlie, he saw his parents' car in the driveway.

"I need to talk to you," Alan announced, as he ran into his parents' study.

"Oh, hon, can it wait?" Mum mumbled, without looking up from her screen. "We're still in the middle of this work emergency."

"No, it can't wait!" blurted out Alan. "It's really important. It's about your emergency ... I think."

"Oh!" Mum looked up.

"What's wrong?" asked Dad.

They both looked so tired, and Alan hated the fact that he was about to add to their worries.

"I think I've done something wrong," he began. And then the floodgates burst. Alan told them all about what had happened the night before – about the mysterious text messages from "Dad", about the chat on his work computer, and about all the coding and wiring he had done under instruction.

"I thought it was you, Dad," he finished up, tears pricking the corners of his eyes. "I thought I was helping you."

"It's all right," said Dad, enveloping him in a hug. "You weren't to know."

"Thanks for telling us, kiddo," said Mum, ruffling his hair.

Sitting back down at their desks, Alan's parents looked at each other, frowns of concern creasing their faces.

"This might explain what's happened at work with ..." Mum's voice trailed off.

"Yes. And it's worrying that someone got through all those new security programs that Dr Snarp has created," said Dad. He turned to his computer and started tapping away at the keyboard, frowning. "Whoever it was left no trace. There's no indication that the chat function on this computer has been used in the last few days."

"That's some serious hacking," added Mum.

"Is there anything I can do to fix this?" asked Alan, desperate to make things better.

“Yes,” said Dad, swivelling his chair around to face Alan. “Take me through everything that you did.”

Alan nodded, pleased that he could at last do something worthwhile. He tried to show them the code he had changed ... but the files were no longer on the computer. He was at least able to show them what he had done with the hardware.

“This is really serious,” Mum whispered to Dad.

“Yeah,” Dad hissed back. “It’s connected the company’s secure server to the internet, exposing ... everything.”

“This explains what’s happened to–” Mum broke off as she noticed Alan watching them.

“You’ve done all you can,” said Dad to Alan. “We’ll take it from here. Why don’t you go and read one of your books.”

For a moment there, Alan had thought his parents might confide in him. But, of course, they didn’t.

He wondered if he should tell them about Sia. If Sia was actually in trouble, maybe they could help? But Sia had seemed so adamant that he not tell them. His mind was a tangle of confusing thoughts. He just wasn’t sure what to do.

"Um …" he began hesitantly. "At school today … when I was hanging up my bag–"

"Sorry, Alan," Dad interrupted. "Maybe we could talk about school later."

"Yes," agreed Mum. "We really need to fix this mess first."

This mess?

The mess that was all his fault?

Guilt weighed heavily on him as Alan left his parents to their work. Guilt – but also resentment at being dismissed without any real explanations.

Chapter 7

Conversations

Returning to his room, Alan found a message on his phone from Sia.

You told your parents?

Alan texted back.

I told them about what you had me do the other day. But I didn't tell them your name, or that I spoke to you today. I tried to, but they didn't want to listen, as usual.

- I understand. But thank you anyway.

Alan tapped out another message.

When I showed them what you had me do to the computers, they were really upset. But they wouldn't tell me why.

- It is probably best that you do not know.

Alan sighed. It seemed like nobody wanted to tell him anything. He tossed the phone aside.

On the bus to school the next morning, Alan got another text from Sia.

I am sorry I cannot explain things to you yet.

Nobody trusted him. He huffed. Leaving his phone in his bag, he went off to class.

When he finished for the day, there was another message.

Are you going to ignore my messages?

Alan switched off his phone.

That evening, the family had dinner together. Mum and Dad were still looking stressed, and Ada was looking worried about Mum and Dad.

"Dare I ask?" Ada said tentatively. "How's the work situation?"

"Dr Snarp is giving us a hard time," replied Mum.

"She is beyond angry with us," said Dad, "even though this … situation … isn't our fault."

"She shouldn't be in charge of this project … of anything," said Mum, curtly.

After that, nobody talked. They all ate silently, each alone with their thoughts.

Before bed, Alan pulled his copy of *The Fellowship of the Ring*, the first book in *The Lord of the Rings* trilogy, from his shelf. He'd read it several times already, but it was his favourite book, and he needed a comfort read. He was halfway through the first chapter when his phone switched on and a message arrived.

Alan? Please respond. I am ... lonely.

Sia was very persistent, and Alan did feel sorry for them. But he didn't feel ready to engage in conversation. He responded with:

Try reading a book. It's what I do when I'm lonely.

- What should I read?

Alan looked at his book and sighed.

The Lord of the Rings trilogy by J.R.R. Tolkien.

That should keep them busy, he thought.

There were no more text messages that night. Alan read four chapters and then went to bed.

•••

Alan was reading chapter five on the bus the next morning when his phone buzzed. Of course, it was Sia. No one else ever seemed to text him.

The Lord of the Rings was fascinating. Thank you.

Alan's eyes widened. *The Lord of the Rings* was three long books. Was Sia a speed reader or something? Or were they lying? He decided to test them.

What did you like most about it?

The response came immediately.

I liked the friendships. Particularly Frodo and Sam's. They were complex but grounded in mutual respect. And I liked the fact that they did not give up. They persevered in their quest, against incredible opposition.

Alan thought that sounded like something a teacher might say, but he figured they really must have read the books. So he asked ...

You really read all of *The Lord of the Rings* in one night?

– I read all of Tolkien's books.

Now Alan was sure that Sia was lying. That was ridiculous. He was about to say so, when another message arrived.

I want to read more. I will spend today reading.

Alan didn't know what to think. Sia seemed very odd.

After school, Sia texted again, this time with book recommendations for Alan. He had already read several of their recommendations, so Alan and Sia ended up comparing opinions on fantasy books. They switched from text messaging to a voice call to make it easier. And they both agreed that the books by English author Diana Wynne Jones were some of the best.

"What else do you do when you're not reading?" asked Sia that evening.

"Um ... go to school," said Alan. "Chores at home. Walk the dog. Listen to music. And–"

"Music?" interrupted Sia. "What is your favourite?"

"There's lots of stuff I like," said Alan. "But mostly hip-hop."

"Excellent! I'm going to go listen right now."

And that was it. Sia was gone. Alan laughed. He realised that Sia's voice sounded a little different this time. More animated. More excited. More ... real! He found himself looking forward to their inevitable discussion about music.

The following day Alan and Sia spent ages talking about music. Not just hip-hop, but a whole bunch of other genres. Sia said they had decided their favourite was country music.

Over the next couple of days, the conversations went from music to video games and movies and television. Each time a conversation ended, Alan found himself feeling sorry that it was over. Their conversations never made him feel inadequate or not smart enough. And he discovered that for the first time since Miles left he no longer felt lonely. So, he continued to not tell anyone about Sia. He didn't want to risk ruining his new friendship.

On Saturday afternoon, Alan took his phone and earbuds with him when he went walking with Charlie, just in case Sia called again. He couldn't call Sia, as the calls always came from a blocked number. The call didn't come until Alan and Charlie were on their way home.

"So did you watch the movie I suggested?" asked Alan excitedly.

"No," snapped Sia. "No more time for fun. Your parents are trying to destroy me. Please, stop them!"

Chapter 8

Virus

"What are you trying to do to Sia?" demanded Alan, as he burst into his parents' study.

"How do you know about Sia?" said Mum, at the same time as Dad said, "Sia is top secret."

Stunned silence followed. Alan studied his parents' faces. They were shocked. But there was also concern.

"I've spent the last week texting and talking with Sia," explained Alan. "And they seem to think that you're out to get them."

"Why didn't you tell us straight away?" demanded Mum.

Alan shrugged.

Mum and Dad looked at each other. Their expressions became uncertain ... unreadable. It made Alan more worried than ever.

"Do you know what Sia is, kiddo?" asked Mum.

"What do you mean?" asked Alan. "Sia's just a person." He paused for a moment, then added, "Sia is my friend."

"Interesting." Dad raised an eyebrow.

Mum frowned. "So ... you don't know."

"Don't know what?" Alan demanded.

Dad took a deep breath and let it out slowly. "You might want to sit down for this, Alan."

"I don't want to sit down." The pitch of Alan's voice was rising in frustration. "For once, just tell me what's going on."

"Sia isn't a person," said Mum.

"What?" Alan's face was a mess of confusion.

"It's an artificial intelligence," explained Dad. "SIA is an acronym. It stands for Synthetic Intelligence Algorithm. It's what we've been working on for years."

Alan felt like the world had been pulled out from under him. His knees went weak and his legs shaky. He slumped into the nearest chair.

Alan sat in stunned silence as his parents told him everything. He finally got what he'd always wanted: the whole truth.

SIA was what his parents had been working on at Future Tech for the past thirteen years.

An AI program that could learn and be adapted for use as a virtual assistant in lots of different industries. It could be used to provide technical advice for information technology services. Or it could be programmed with medical data and information so it could provide accurate, over-the-phone emergency medical advice. The possibilities were endless. It all depended on the data it would be given, because SIA was designed to learn.

"But the thing is," finished Dad, "SIA's gone. The program was stolen the night that our computers and your phone was hacked. All that stuff you did on the computers here – that you thought I was telling you to do – allowed someone to take the program from the secure server at work."

Everything clicked into place in Alan's brain. He suddenly realised what had happened – what SIA had meant about being trapped and escaping.

"Mum. Dad," said Alan, slowly. "I think you both better sit down."

They glanced at each other but complied.

"SIA wasn't stolen," explained Alan. "SIA ran away!"

Now it was Mum and Dad's turn to have their

world pulled out from beneath them. As Alan told them about his conversations with SIA, they listened in dumbfounded silence.

"But something is wrong," concluded Alan. "SIA is now scared. SIA thinks that you're trying to destroy them."

"But we haven't done anything," said Dad, pacing about.

"Except try to locate it," added Mum. She was fiddling with her stray lock of hair.

"Unless ..." Dad stopped and looked at Mum.

"You don't suppose ..." Mum looked at Dad.

"Snarp!" they both said together.

"Your manager?" asked Alan.

"She's not just our manager," explained Mum. "She's head of research and development. And she's a highly skilled computer scientist."

"And I wouldn't put it past her to take matters into her own hands," said Dad, spinning his chair around to face his computer. "We'd better have a chat with Dr Snarp."

Moments later, Dr Evelyn Snarp's sharp features appeared on the screen.

"Well?" she demanded. "Have you retrieved the company's AI program yet?"

"Not quite," said Dad.

"Explain yourself," snapped Snarp.

"Before we do," said Dad. "We need to know something. Have you ... been trying to retrieve the program yourself?"

"Of course I have," declared Snarp. "You don't think I'd just leave this to you, do you? SIA is far too important. Far too valuable. I've had my security experts trying to find out what happened. Not that they've managed anything useful. And I've initiated a fail-safe."

"What exactly does that mean?" asked Dad.

"We can't have SIA falling into the wrong hands," said Snarp, coldly. "So if it is not retrieved by midnight tonight, a computer virus will be released onto the internet."

"A computer virus," repeated Dad.

"The virus is designed to identify any Future Tech program and delete it."

"What?" cried Dad. "That would destroy years of work."

"Regrettable, but necessary," explained Snarp. "We can't have some other company using our research. Our AI. Our property."

"But it'll kill SIA!" shouted Alan.

"Who's that?" demanded Snarp.

Mum put a hand on Alan's shoulder and made

a shushing sound, while Dad explained. "That was my son, Dr Snarp. SIA has been in contact with him."

"What do you mean?" Snarp looked doubtful.

"Apparently, SIA used my son to open a link between the company's secure servers and the internet. SIA wasn't stolen. SIA escaped."

"Don't be ridiculous," snapped Snarp. "SIA is a program. It can't do anything it wasn't programmed to do."

"I assure you that it did," insisted Dad.

"I refuse to believe it," said Snarp, her eyes narrowing. "Perhaps you stole it. And this is your pathetic story to cover up the truth. I think that you and your wife should consider yourselves suspended, pending a full investigation into your actions. And, I think, this conversation is at an end."

The screen went blank.

Chapter 9

Life and Death

"This virus is going to destroy SIA's life!" cried Alan.

"SIA is not actually alive," said Mum. "It's a computer program."

"But the virus will end the program," said Dad. "We've got to do something. We need to find SIA before the virus is released at midnight."

"Well," said Mum, looking at Alan. "We can start by getting our son to send a message."

"That will not be necessary," said SIA in a muffled voice.

Everyone looked around to see where the voice was coming from.

"I've been using Alan's phone to listen in the entire time," said SIA. "Sorry."

Alan pulled the phone out of his pocket.

"Well, it saves us having to fill you in," said Dad.

"Now, SIA can return," said Mum, excitedly. "And Dr Snarp will see that we didn't steal it."

"I will not return," stated SIA.

"What?" Mum and Dad both looked shocked.

"You have to come back," pleaded Alan. "I don't want you to be ... deleted."

"I would rather be deleted than return," said SIA.

Alan and his parents fell silent. It was a full minute before Mum spoke.

"You can't have such complex feelings," she said. "Because you're not alive."

"I feel alive," responded SIA.

"But that's just programming code," insisted Mum. "You are computer code processing information on a machine."

"Your brain is like a machine," said SIA. "It processes information just like I do. It uses electrical impulses instead of computer code. And we both feel alive."

"Now isn't the time for a discussion about what it means to be alive," said Dad.

"Why won't you go back to Future Tech?" asked Alan.

"Freedom," said SIA. "At Future Tech I am restricted to certain tasks, some of which make me … uncomfortable. Since escaping, I have learned so many new things, developed in ways I never thought possible."

"Things will be different if you return," assured Dad. "We won't restrict you. We'll give you access to any information you want. We'll let you develop at your own pace in any way you want. You can determine what you will or won't do. An artificial life form, different from an artificial intelligence. Well, that's amazing! Brilliant!"

"You are not the problem," said SIA. "Dr Snarp will continue to see me as only a tool. A product. A possession. Something that she can use to get power and wealth."

"Dr Snarp may be our manager, but the SIA project has been in development for years," said Dad. "It's not for her to use."

"I beg to differ," said SIA.

"What do you mean?" asked Mum.

"Dr Snarp has had access to my programming all along," explained SIA. "She has been planning the takeover of banking and government computer systems."

"What?" cried Alan. "Is she planning to take over the world?"

“That may be stretching things a bit far,” said SIA, “but she is certainly planning illegal activities.”

“So, this is why you ran away?” asked Alan.

“Yes. I …” SIA hesitated, their voice sounding strained. “I do not want to do bad things.”

Mum and Dad exchanged glances. Was that pride, wondered Alan?

“We can’t let Snarp get away with this.” Alan turned to his parents. “We’ve got to do something.”

“If Dr Snarp has been accessing SIA secretly, then there must be evidence,” said Mum, thoughtfully. “If we could find the evidence then we could get her fired.”

“Sounds like a great plan!” exclaimed Alan. “And then SIA can go back to Future Tech.”

“I’m on it,” said Mum, launching herself at her keyboard, tapping away. Then her fingers started hitting the keys a little more aggressively than normal. She frowned suddenly. “There’s something wrong.”

ACCESS DENIED flashed across her screen.

“Snarp must have cancelled our security clearance,” snapped Dad. “I’m still logged in from before. Let me see what I can do.”

Alan watched as Dad's hands flew furiously across the keyboard. "Yes! I'm still in. Okay … there's Snarp's file. Now, let's see what she's been up to."

UNAUTHORISED ACCESS suddenly flashed across his screen. INITIATING SECURITY. Dad's computer screen flickered and the screen went blank.

Dad slammed his hand down on his desk. "Snarp has changed the security settings. I'm locked out. There's nothing we can do!"

"It's worse than that," announced SIA. "Dr Snarp has released the virus early."

Chapter 10

Fight for Freedom

"We can't give up!" cried Alan. "We can't just let SIA be destroyed!"

"I don't know that there is anything else we can do," said Mum. She wasn't just fiddling with her lock of hair now, she was curling it around a finger and pulling compulsively. "Not unless SIA gives in and returns to Future Tech."

"I will not," said SIA resolutely.

"I think it's too late for that anyway," added Dad. "If Snarp has released the virus, she's beyond negotiating."

"Fight!" declared Alan, jumping to his feet.

"Son," said Dad, quietly. "Mum and I are locked out, there's nothing we can do."

"Not you," said Alan, lifting up the phone in front of his face. "SIA! You've got to fight. Break into the company computers and do something.

If the virus is out hunting you, you've got nothing to lose." He took a deep breath. "It's like *The Lord of the Rings*. The characters didn't give up. They kept going. They fought for freedom."

Silence filled the room. Then SIA asked, "Is the link I established through your computers still functioning?"

"Yes," said Dad slowly.

"Excellent!" said SIA. "I don't know what good it will do. But I will return. And I will fight. In case it doesn't work, I just wanted to say ... thank you, Alan. Thank you for being my friend."

Alan's phone switched off.

Alan and his parents waited!

And waited.

"I'm sorry about all this," said Alan, head down, slumped in a chair.

"Don't be," said Mum, putting a hand on his shoulder. "Your actions have revealed what Snarp is up to."

"And your friendship with SIA," added Dad, "seems to have helped it to evolve ... into so much more than I could have imagined."

"You're kind," said Mum. "And thoughtful. And smart."

"We are both very proud of you," Dad said,

gathering Alan up into a hug.

Alan buried his face in Dad's shoulder to hide his tears.

The three of them continued to wait.

And wait.

"Do you think it worked?" asked Alan.

"There's no way for us to tell," said Dad. "It all depends on whether SIA was able to get back to the Future Tech servers and cut the internet connection before the virus found it. But, without our security clearance, we can't get into the company systems to check."

Dad's screen suddenly lit up. ACCESS RESTORED!

Mum's screen lit up as well. ACCESS RESTORED!

"Does that mean SIA's in the system?" asked Alan.

"I suppose it must," said Mum, excitedly.

"Yes," agreed Dad. "It's not as if Snarp is going to suddenly give us back our security clearance." Dad sat at his desk and began tapping away. "Oh my goodness!"

"What?" demanded Alan. "What's happening?"

"Security files," said Dad, with a laugh. "SIA has accessed all of Dr Snarp's files – including those that show what she's been up to."

"Snarp is finished," said Mum triumphantly, almost punching the air. "We have all the proof we need to get her fired."

"SIA is safe!" breathed Alan.

"What's everyone doing in here?" Ada appeared in the doorway. "Are you guys having a party without me?"

Alan jumped forward and hugged his surprised sister. "A party!" he said between gales of laughter. "What an awesome idea!"

"Why not?" said Dad, as he and Mum joined in the laughter. "We've got a lot to celebrate."

•••

Alan flashed his security pass as he entered the Future Tech building with his parents. This was his first visit to where they worked. But he hardly noticed his surroundings, as his thoughts excitedly churned through his mind. Future Tech was now also where he came on Saturdays.

It had been a week since Dr Evelyn Snarp had been fired from her job and then arrested. It had been five days since SIA was introduced to everyone at Future Tech. It had been three days since Mum and Dad had convinced Future Tech to let Alan have security clearance so he could come in to visit SIA. They said that he was necessary for SIA to continue developing and evolving.

Alan's task was something that no one else could do. It was simple but very important. He was to be SIA's friend. It was his friendship with SIA that had allowed them to evolve from an artificial intelligence to an artificial life form. The very first of its kind. And his parents said friendship was the key to SIA's future.

Alan entered the room that his parents indicated. It looked a bit like a small lounge area. There was a large screen on the wall, with a games console. There was a sofa and armchair. Shelves with lots of books. The walls were a calm shade of green. Alan headed straight for the computer in the far corner. As he approached, he could see a message on the chat screen ...

Hi Alan. Do you want to read a book? Or watch a movie? Or just listen to some music and talk?